Mandy Shaw's Redwork Christmas

Over 15 Festive Redwork Projects

Dandelion Designs Publications

love
Mandy
x

Contents

I dedicate this book to the latest addition
to our family Denny. Your smiles and giggles
fill us all with such joy, you are a delight,
just like your Mum.

Festive Greetings!

Whatever time of the year you are reading this, may I send you my warmest Christmas best wishes? Welcome to a collection of redwork stitchery that will keep you busy until Christmas Eve, and truly put you in the mood for mince pies, cosy fire sides, carol singing and Yuletide cheer.

Christmas is my favourite time of the year, and I allow myself free and unfettered rein to fill my home with decorations designed to make it the most welcoming sanctuary for family returning from far and wide and lovely visiting friends. Redwork embroidery is perfect for Christmas stitchery, given that it is almost always worked in glorious red thread. I use an irresistible coton à broder and the best fabrics I can find, usually linen. Redwork embroidery itself has a long and noble history, beginning in Britain and boosted by its adoption by American stitchers. To trace that history we must go back right back to the beginning, to the birth of the School of Art Needlework in 1872. The word 'royal' was only added in 1875 when Queen Victoria consented to become its first patron.

Just after the founding of the Royal School of Needlework, in 1876, a world fair was held in Philadelphia, USA. Fairs such as this were hugely popular, and were held to show off to the world the host nation's culture, new inventions and new scientific advancements. The fair in Philadelphia was the first of its kind in America, and it boasted a wide range of exhibits from Heinz ketchup to Alexander Graham Bell's telephone. The Royal School of Needlework showcased its work at the fair with a type of simple surface embroidery, hand sewn with a backstitch then known as the Kensington stitch, named after the school's location in London. The Americans loved this new technique and started to embroider designs with simple outlines to decorate household wares.

At around the same time a new but expensive synthetic dye, Turkey red, was developed and became highly prized for its durability. It had the advantage of being colourfast, meaning it would not bleed or run or fade. It owes its name to the fact that 'Turkey' was the catch-all term used for the Middle East at the time, where the dye was made. The dyeing process was long and complicated, and even today red is an expensive dye to produce.

This new red thread and the inspiration from the Royal School of Needlework led to the explosion of simple outline designs on a white background embroidered in red, which became known as redwork.

And so my favourite embroidery technique was born! And in this book, I've brought it together with my favourite season to give you a gathering of gorgeous projects with a wealth of designs to choose from.

Happy Christmas stitching!

Six Mini
Decorations

Six Mini Decorations

Deck your halls with decorations — or your tree, or the knobs on your kitchen cupboards, or anywhere else you feel deserves a little bit of extra festive cheer. These little lovelies are simple to make but do include an unusual technique so follow the instructions carefully and all will be fine. Choose from half a dozen Christmas characters, or make them all and add a cheerful red ribbon to match your stitchery so you can hang them up all around your home.

YOU WILL NEED
(to make all six)

* 11 x 42in (28cm x 1.05m) linen or cotton fabric, white
* 11 x 27in (28cm x 69cm) light-weight iron-on interfacing
* Coton à broder or embroidery floss, red
* Chenille 24 needle
* Small bag of stuffing
* Thread to match fabric
* 3¾yd (3m) ribbon

Finished size approx: 5 x 3in (12.5 x 7.5cm)
or 4 x 4in (10 x 10cm) each

1 Cut two squares or rectangles of fabric roughly the right size, but larger than your chosen redwork design (see templates on pages 12-13) by about an inch (2.5cm) all around.

2 Transfer your redwork design on to the right side of one piece of fabric (see Transferring a Design). Set the other piece aside to become the backing.

3 Iron on the interfacing to the wrong side of fabric with the design on it, this will stabilise it and prevent stray threads from showing on the right side.

4 Embroider the design with a back stitch (see Essential Stitches) and the coton à broder, or use two strands of embroidery floss. Sew French knots for the musical notes and at the points of the triangles on the drum design, and for the eye of the robin, make star stitches around the fairy and the robin, and use cross stitches inside each scallop in the border (see Essential Stitches). Press.

5 Place the embroidered fabric and the backing fabric right sides together.

6 Use a hand back stitch or a sewing machine to sew the two pieces together ¹⁄₁₆in (2mm) from the outside edge of the embroidered scallop border. Sew all the way around leaving *no* gap.

> Leaving a gap when you sew up a project, once stuffed, always leaves a crooked seam so I have a better idea... see step 8 and then steps 10 to 12.
>
> Mandy's Top Tip

7 Trim the shape ¼in (5mm) from the sewn edge. If making a heart-shaped decoration, cut across the point at the bottom of the heart and snip into the heart's 'cleavage' – all of this creates a nice heart shape once stuffed.

8 On the wrong side of the decoration, make a horizontal 1in (2.5cm) cut, 1in (2.5cm) down from the top. Turn the decoration the right way out.

9 Sew with coton à broder or embroidery thread, using a back stitch, through all the layers on the inside line of the scallops. Because the border design has already been embroidered the back stitch will not show. This will create the decorative edge.

10 Stuff firmly. Ladder stitch the slit in the back closed (see Essential Stitches).

11 Cut the ribbon into six equal pieces. Use one piece of ribbon for each decoration. Cut each piece in two, then fold one of the pieces in half and slightly cross over the ribbon half way down. Stitch to the top of the back of the decoration.

12 With the other half of the ribbon tie a bow and sew this on the back of the decoration. This bow will cover the stuffing slit with a nice flourish.

Six Mini Decorations

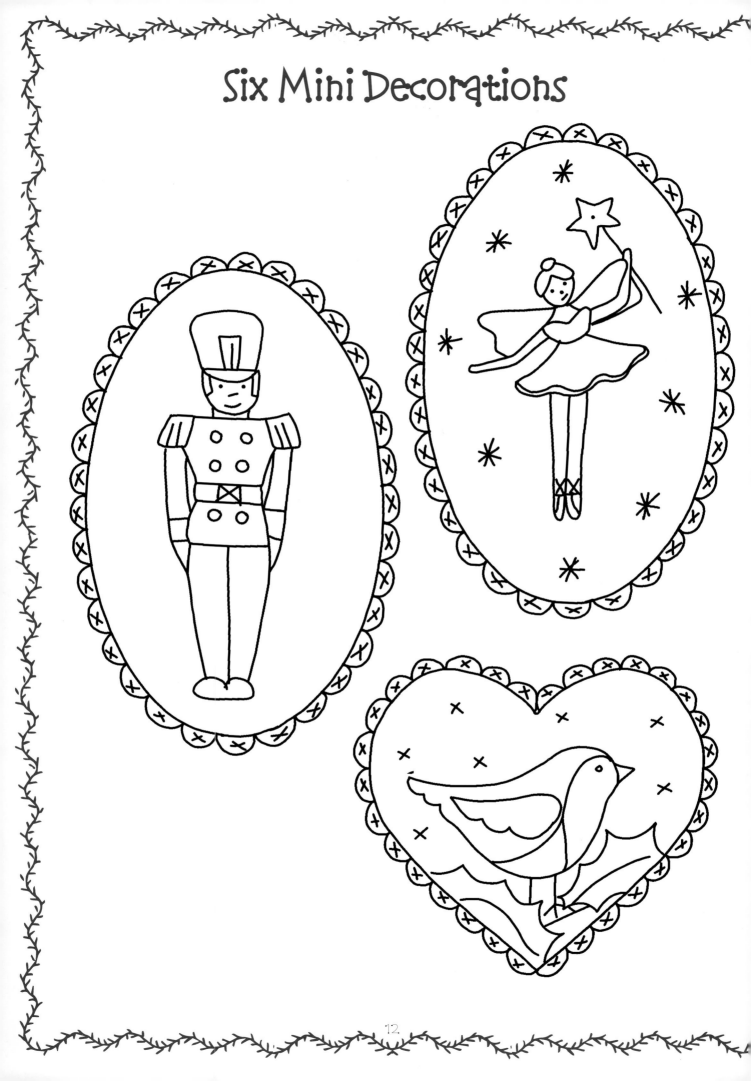

Six Mini Decorations

Snow Dome
Cushion

Snow Dome Cushion

A snowy scene of cosy houses is the perfect design for this Christmas cushion. If you turn it upside down and shake it, the snow really swirls about! Well, alright, not really, but if you've ever collected snow domes or owned one as a child, you can summon up a little nostalgic magic and imagine the drifting snowflakes as you enjoy a glass of sherry and a post-luncheon snooze on the sofa.

YOU WILL NEED
* 7 x 7in (18 x 18cm) linen, white
* 13 x 21in (33 x 52.5cm) fabric, red
* 3 x 45in (7.5cm x 1.1m) linen mix fabric, grey
* Thread to match linen fabric
* Coton à broder, red
* Chenille 24 needle
* 48in (1.2m) fabric-covered piping, red
* 14 x 14in (35.5 x 35.5cm) wadding
* Spray adhesive (optional)
* 14 x 14in (35.5 x 35.5cm) cushion pad

Finished size approx: 12 x 12in (30 x 30cm)

1 Trim the white linen to an accurate 6½ x 6½in (16.5 x 16.5cm) square. Transfer the snow dome design onto the fabric (see template on page 18 and Transferring a Design).

2 To make the cushion front, cut two strips of red fabric 1½ x 6½in (4 x 16.5cm), and two strips 1½ x 8½in (4 x 22cm). Sew the shorter strips to the top and bottom of the white linen square, and the longer ones on each side, all with a ¼in (5mm) seam. Press.

3 Cut two strips of grey fabric 2½ x 8½in (6.5 x 22cm), and two more strips measuring 2½ x 12½in (6.5 x 32cm).

4 Sew the shorter strips to the top and bottom and the longer ones to each side of your cushion front, again with a ¼in (5mm) seam. Press.

5 Tack the wadding to the wrong side or use spray adhesive (see Spray Adhesive). Add a line of running stitch in coton à broder around the cushion about ½in (1cm) from the seam between the red and grey borders (see main photograph).

6 Stitch the snow dome design with a back stitch (see Essential Stitches) and coton à broder. Add a star stitch to the top of the Christmas tree in the design, and cross stitches to the roof of the

Always use coton à broder as it comes off the skein, without trying to divide it. It is not stranded like embroidery floss.

Mandy's Top Tip

central house and either side of the 'Merry Christmas' greeting (see Essential Stitches).

7 Sew the piping cord to the edge of the cushion, starting half way down one side. Line up the edge of the piping with the edge of the front of the cushion. Use a zipper foot on your sewing machine and stitch as close to the 'hump' of the piping as possible.

8 When you come to the corner snip into the flat part of the piping and go around the corner, not into the point of the corner. When you come to the beginning again turn the end of the piping 'off' the cushion.

9 Cut two rectangles of red fabric, 12 x 9in (30 x 23cm). Hem one long side of both pieces by turning under ½in (1cm) and then another ½in (1cm), press and stitch the folds in place. Place one rectangle over the other so that they overlap, with the hemmed sides nearest the centre. Adjust the overlap until the rectangles together cover an area of 12 x 12in (30 x 30cm). Pin this to the cushion front, right sides together, and sew around the outside edge by machine, sewing on the same line as the one you sewed the piping on. Snip your corners and trim the seams. Machine zig zag stitch over the seam to prevent fraying. Turn the right way out and fill with the cushion pad.

Snow Dome Cushion

×Merry Christmas×

Bauble
Hanging
Heart

Bauble Hanging Heart

Hanging hearts are a favourite of mine, and this one is no exception. A trio of baubles fills the heart-shape so perfectly it's as if they were meant to be. If Christmas has brought out your creative sparkle you can come up with your own personal bauble design. Look out for my satisfyingly simple 'secret stuffing closure technique' to ensure you get a perfect finish.

YOU WILL NEED
✷ 10 x 10in (25 x 25cm) white linen or cotton fabric
✷ 10 x 10in (25 x 25cm) red check fabric for backing
✷ 10 x 10in (25 x 25cm) light-weight iron-on interfacing
✷ Coton à broder or embroidery floss, red
✷ Chenille 24 needle
✷ Handful of toy stuffing
✷ Thread to match fabric
✷ 1yd (1m) of ½in (1cm) wide ribbon

Finished size approx: 6 x 7in (15 x 18cm)

1 Transfer the hanging heart design onto the right side of the white linen or cotton (see template on page 25 and Transferring a Design).

2 Iron on the interfacing to the wrong side of this piece of fabric. This will stabilise it and prevent stray threads from showing on the right side.

3 Embroider the stitch design with a back stitch (see Essential Stitches). Don't forget to stitch the scalloped border design too. Add French knots in the 'squiggle pattern' on the top left bauble and running stitch in the two bands across it. Make cross stitches in the two bands on the top right bauble, and larger cross stitches in the three circles on the bottom bauble, as shown. Then work a French knot in each scallop in the border design (see Essential Stitches). Sew with two strands of embroidery floss or one of coton à broder. Press.

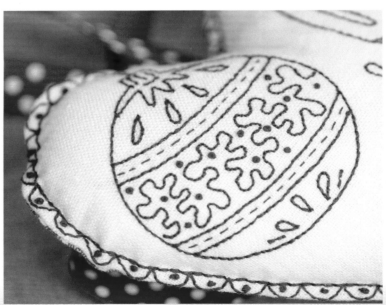

4 Next place the finished embroidered fabric and the backing fabric right sides together.

5 Use a hand back stitch or a sewing machine to sew the two pieces together, 1/16 in (2mm) from the outside edge of the embroidered scallop. Sew all the way around leaving no gap. Sewing a gap once stuffed always leaves a crooked seam so try my method for perfect results.

6 Trim the heart shape ¼in (5mm) from the sewn edge. Cut the excess fabric across the point at the bottom of the heart and snip into the heart's 'cleavage,' all of this creates a nice heart shape once stuffed.

7 Cut a 1½in (4cm) horizontal slit, 1½in (4cm) down from the top edge of the wrong side of the backing fabric heart only. This will be your slit for stuffing the heart. Turn the right way out.

8 Back stitch with embroidery thread through all the layers on the inside line of the scallops. This has already been embroidered but the back stitch will not show. This will create the decorative edge to the hanging heart.

9 Stuff firmly. Ladder stitch the slit closed (see Essential Stitches).

10 Cut the ribbon into two equal pieces. Using one piece of ribbon, fold in half and slightly cross over the ribbon half way down.

11 Stitch though the point where the ribbon crosses, onto the back of the heart to attach it where the stuffing slit is.

12 With the other half of the ribbon tie a bow and sew this on the heart, just below where the first ribbon crosses. This decoration will neatly cover the slit you used for stuffing.

Bauble Hanging Heart

Festive
Mini Bunting

Festive Mini Bunting

Bunting makes everything better! Hang it in the hall, string it up the stairs, loop it round your lounge, or drape it in the drawing room (if you're posh). Personally, I like a bit of bunting on the mantelpiece, but I do secure it well so it doesn't dangle too close to the fire. I've depicted things that make me feel festive, but you can adjust the design to personalise it.

YOU WILL NEED
* 18 x 22in (46 x 55cm) linen, white
* 10 x 9in (25 x 23cm) light-weight iron-on interfacing
* Coton à broder, red
* Chenille 24 needle
* 30in (75cm) bias binding
* Thread to match fabric
*8 small buttons, white linen-covered

Finished size approx: 30in (75cm) long

1 Using the template opposite and the white linen, cut out two triangles for each flag (cut triangles for as many flags as you require). A seam allowance of ¼in (5mm) is included in the template. Next cut the same number of triangles from the interfacing.

2 Transfer the designs onto the right side of the flags (see opposite and Transferring a Design). Place the interfacing on the wrong side and iron on.

3 Embroider the designs using back stitch and coton à broder. Work French knots for the eyes of the birds, snowman and chorister, and the musical notes around the chorister's head. Make star stitches around the word 'Joy' (see Essential Stitches).

4 When you have stitched the design, place another white linen triangle over your stitching, so the two pieces are right sides together. Sew around the edges of the two long sides with a ¼in (5mm) seam. Leave the top side open. Turn the flag the right way out and press gently.

5 Open out the bias binding, leave 6in (15cm) at one end before the first flag. Line up the raw edge of the binding with the raw edge of the right side of the flag. Leave a ½in (1cm) gap between the flags. Sew the flags in place by sewing in the fold of the binding. Once all of the flags are in place, turn the binding over to the wrong side and slip stitch in place. I also top stitched (see Essential Stitches) the binding from the front so it laid nice and flat. Sew one white button between each flag.

The embroidery can be done before you sew the two sides of the flags together, but if you are adding buttons these are best done afterwards as they may interfere with sewing the seams together.

Mandy's Top Tip

Festive Mini Bunting

Joy

Seam Allowance

Santa's Sleigh Placemats

Santa's Sleigh Placemats

On Dasher, on Dancer, on Prancer and Vixen! On Comet, on Cupid, on Donner and Blitzen! On your list of 'Things I Must Stitch Before December 25th', then onto your table to put a smile on everyone's face as you serve up Christmas lunch. Look out for the simple method for adding borders and using them to bind the edges of the placemats.

YOU WILL NEED
* 13 x 42in (33cm x 1.05m) cream osnaburg fabric
* 13 x 42in (33cm x 1.05m) wadding
* 13 x 42in (33cm x 1.05m) red backing fabric
* 13 x 14in (33 x 35.5cm) of four different fabrics for borders
* Spray adhesive (optional)
* Coton à broder, red
* Chenille 24 needle
* 4yd (3.6m) ric rac, red
* Sewing thread, red

Finished size approx: 12½ x 10½in (32 x 27cm)

1 Cut out four 12½ x 10½in (32 x 27cm) rectangles from the cream osnaburg fabric and four of the same size from the red backing and the wadding.

All seam allowances have been added to the measurements for these placemats.

Mandy's Top Tip

2 Transfer the designs onto the centre of the osnaburg rectangles of fabric (see Templates and Transferring a Design).

3 Pin or spray glue the wadding to the wrong side of the design (see Spray Adhesive).

4 Embroider each design with a back stitch and make the reindeer eyes with star stitches and Father Christmas's eyes with French knots (see Essential Stitches), using coton à broder.

5 Draw a line 1½in (4cm) from the edge, around all four sides of each mat.

6 Place the ric rac on each of the four sides, lining up the middle of the ric rac with the line you have drawn. Cut each piece of ric rac separately – accuracy is important here so do take your time to get it right. Sew the ric rac on, straight down the middle, using red thread.

7 Cut each piece of red fabric into four strips 3½in (9cm) wide. These will be attached to the side of the design. To get the ric rac perfectly positioned, place the borders on top of the ric rac, right sides together, with the raw edge of the fabric matching the edge of the sewn on ric rac. Sew with a perfect ¼in (5mm) seam. You should have little humps of ric rac showing on the right side of the placemat (see photograph below).

8 Attach the strips to make the border by starting on one side and sewing a strip to each edge

in turn (see tip). Press each strip back before sewing on the next one and trim off the excess fabric in line with the edge of the cream fabric when you get to each end. It will look odd but will work out fine.

9 Top stitch the border fabric on the right side around each mat, ¼in (5mm) from the seam with the cream osnaburg fabric (see photograph).

10 Spray glue or tack the backing to the wrong side of the mat (see Spray Adhesive).

11 Press the borders to the wrong side of each mat, turn under a ½in (1cm) seam and hand sew each border to the reverse of the mat. To mitre the corners, fold the border on one side over the wrong side, press and pin. Prepare the next side in the same manner but fold down the corner at a 45 degree angle, before you fold it over completely. Turn under a ½in (6mm) seam before you slip stitch it in place.

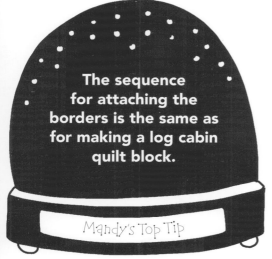

The sequence for attaching the borders is the same as for making a log cabin quilt block.

Mandy's Top Tip

Santa's Sleigh Placemats

Santa's Sleigh Placemats

Santa's Sleigh Placemats

Santa's Sleigh Placemats

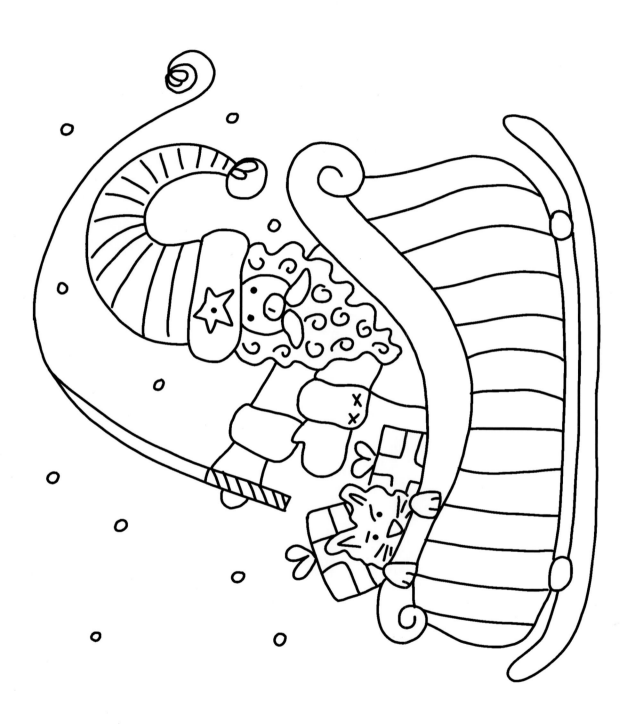

Forty Winks Bolster Cushion

Forty Winks Bolster Cushion

Why not showcase your beautiful redwork with this festive bolster? This little scene shows Father Christmas himself putting his feet up by the fire after an exhausting night of present delivery. I wonder who fills his stocking? If you've never made a bolster cushion before, don't panic, you'll find lots of useful tips here on how to create the shape, make neat ends and fit the zip.

YOU WILL NEED
✱ 14 x 9in (35.5 x 23cm) linen, natural coloured
✱14 x 9in (35.5 x 23cm) light-weight iron-on interfacing
✱ 10 x 45in (26cm x 1.1m) circle-print fabric
✱ 20 x 45in (50cm x 1.1m) striped red fabric
✱ 9 x 45in (23cm x 1.1m) striped cream fabric
✱ 9 x 12in (23 x 30cm) coral-print fabric
✱ 20 x 30in (50 x 75cm) cotton-mix wadding
✱ Coton à broder, red and cream
✱ Chenille 24 needle
✱ Sewing threads to match linen and striped fabric
✱ 2 plastic domes or self-covered buttons, 2in (50mm)
✱ 20in (50cm) continuous zip
✱ 18 x 8in (46 x 20 no.4 piping cord
18in x 18in (46 x 20cm) bolster cushion

Finished size approx: 18 x 8in (46 x 20cm)

• Please note that when you are working with the striped fabric be careful to check the direction of the stripe.

Mandy's Top Tips

1 Transfer the embroidery design onto the linen fabric (see template on pages 46–47 and Transferring a Design).

2 Iron on the interfacing to the wrong side to help stabilise the fabric whilst you are working it.

3 Embroider the design in back stitch using red coton à broder, making the cat's and Father Christmas's eyes with French knots, and working star stitches on the tinsel on the Christmas tree and round the fireplace (see Essential Stitches).

4 Once the embroidery is sewn, trim the work to 13½ x 7½in (34 x 19cm).

5 Cut two strips of circle-print fabric 13½ x 1½in (34 x 4cm) and sew them to the top and bottom of the embroidery. Press them back. Cut two more strips 9½ x 1½in (24 x 4cm) and sew these to the two sides, then press.

6 Cut two 2 x 15½in (5 x 39.5cm) strips of red striped fabric and sew them to the top and bottom of the work, press. Cut two more red striped fabric strips 2 x 12½in (5 x 32cm) and sew to the sides.

7 Cut a 18½ x 2½in (47 x 6.5cm) strip in coral-print fabric and sew it to the top of your work.

8 Cut six 3½in (9cm) squares in circle-print fabric, three in red striped fabric and nine in cream striped fabric. Join these together using the diagram on page 42 as a guide. Press well and join to the last strip.

9 Cut another 18½ x 2½in (6.5cm) strip in coral-print fabric and sew this to the other side of your squares.

10 Lay this piece of patchwork onto the wadding and either tack in place or glue with spray adhesive (see Spray Adhesive).

I didn't use a backing fabric as a lining for the bolster cover as it is only a cushion so the inside won't get too much wear and tear.

Mandy's Top Tips

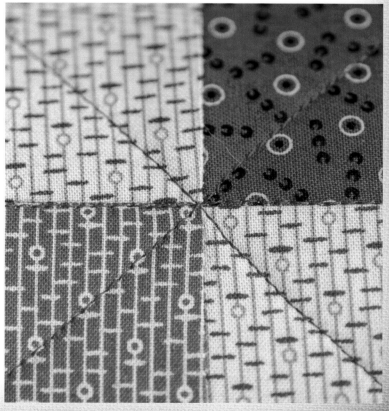

Forty winks sewing plan

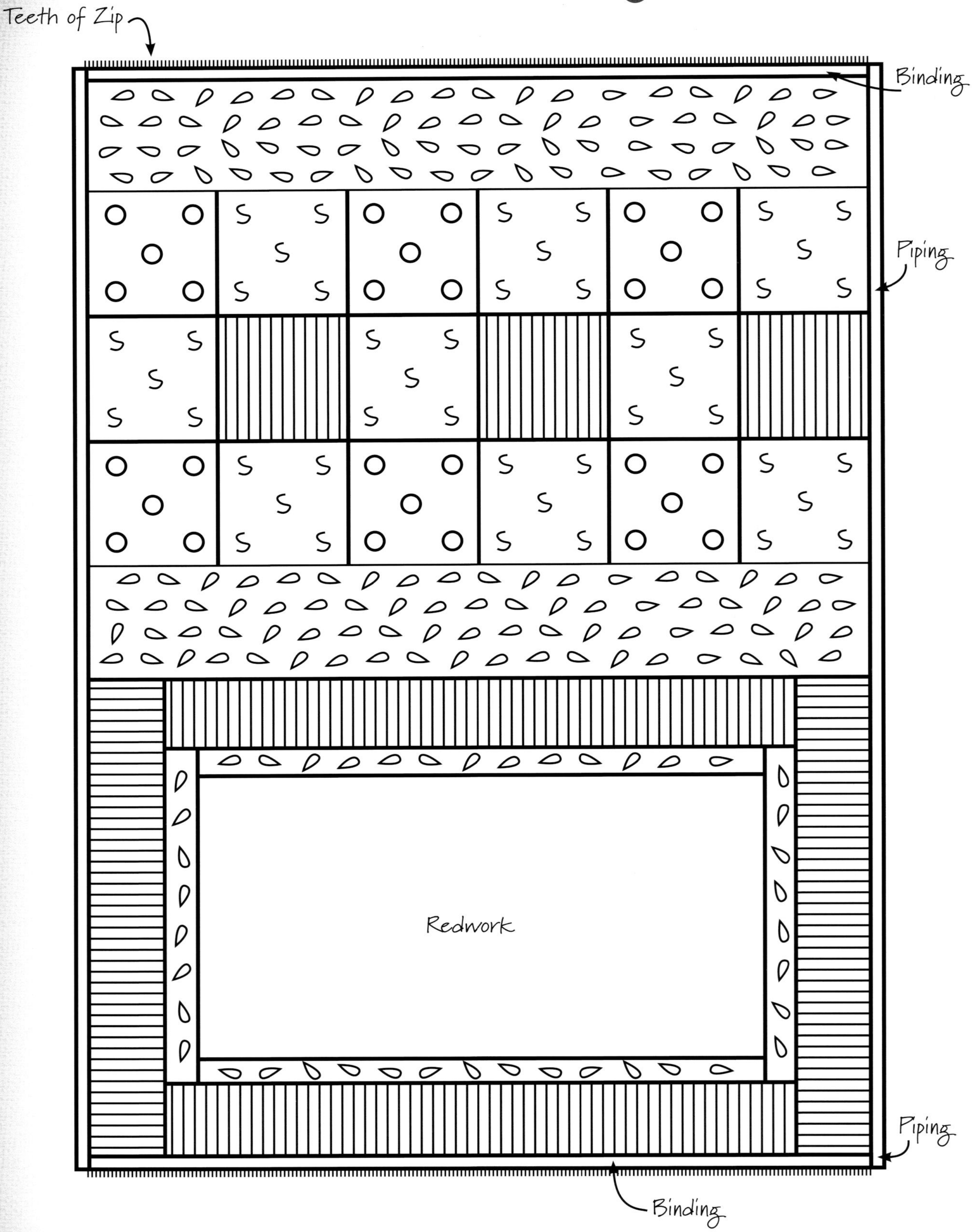

Teeth of Zip

Binding

Piping

Redwork

Piping

Binding

11 Machine quilt the work, using matching thread, along all the straight seams in the ditch. I also quilted diagonally in both directions across all of the patchwork squares.

12 Hand quilt a free-form wavy line around the red circle-print border in running stitch (see Essential Stitches) using cream coton à broder.

13 Trim the work into a neat rectangle.

14 To make the piping, first cut two 1¼ x 24in (3.25 x 60cm) strips of circle-print fabric. Iron in half, wrong sides together. Pop the piping cord into the fold of the strip and sew as close to the cord as possible with your sewing machine. If you have a piping foot, use this. Lay the prepared piping, raw edge to one side of the cushion, matching the raw edges. Sew the piping on to the side. Repeat with the other side.

15 Next insert the zip. Bind both short ends of the work with the cream striped fabric: cut a strip 1½ x 19½in (4 x 49.5cm), place it right sides together with the cushion front, sew in place with your machine, then take it over to the back to stitch in place. Repeat for the other short end.

16 Open out the continuous zip and sew one side of the zip to the end furthest away from the embroidery. Just place the zipper underneath the bound edge with the teeth protruding to the side, it nestles in nicely, make

sure you have at least ½in (1cm) of zip protruding at each end. From the front, right side, sew another line of stitching with the intention of catching the zip but also for decorative effect.

17 With thread that matches the striped fabric, sew the zip on the other side of the cushion cover, but this time sew it a ¼in (5mm) away from the edge of the binding, as shown.

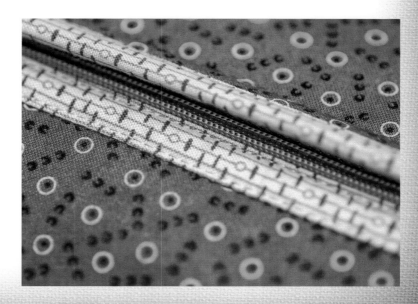

JOINING THE PULL TO THE ZIP

This works like magic and will transform how you work with continuous zips forever! Cut away ½in (1cm) of the teeth on the right side of the zip end. Place the zip pull onto the left side and pull the right side down into the zipper pull. Hold the zip and do the zip up – magic! If it doesn't work you are doing something wrong, so try again.

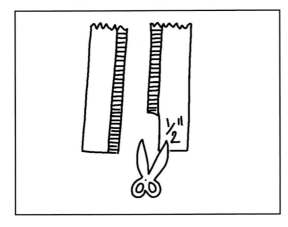

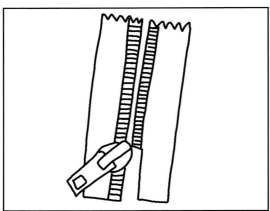

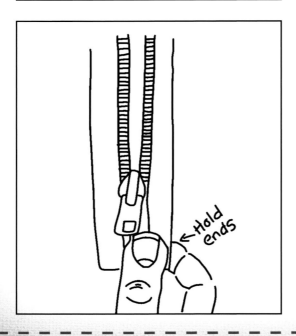

18 Cut two 4 x 24in (10 x 60cm) strips of coral-print fabric and sew one to each side of the bolster, making sure they overhang by ½in (1cm) at each end. You will be incorporating the piping into this seam so do sew as close to the hump of the piping as possible (this might take two attempts!).

19 Do up the zip and the bound edge should overlap nicely. Fold the bolster in half lengthwise, right-sides together, and pin and sew the seam.

20 With double thread sew a line of running stitch ½in (1cm) from the outside edge of each of the bolster ends. Gather up the bolster ends and fasten off securely. The raw edges of the fabric should just be touching.

21 Cut a circle of circle-print fabric out ½in (1cm) bigger than your plastic domes and use running stitch to gather around the dome and pull the fabric up tightly. Glue or sew on the fabric-covered domes to cover up the hole on the ends of the bolster.

22 Pop in the cushion, do up that zip and be proud!

Forty Winks Bolster Cushion

Forty Winks Bolster Cushion

Festive Mayhem Wreath

Festive Mayhem Wreath

Can anything be too Christmassy? I don't think so. Behold my festive mayhem wreath! I've included all my favourite Christmas things, jostling for space in a hoopie, so you can hang them up and enjoy a burst of seasonal cheer every time you glance at them. A hoopie is a great way to display your redwork — why not try the snow dome design from page 14 in a smaller embroidery hoop?

YOU WILL NEED
* 18 x 18in (46 x 46cm) linen fabric, white
* 18 x 18in (46 x 46cm) light-weight iron-on interfacing
* 2 x skeins Coton à broder or embroidery floss, red
* Chenille 24 needle
* Sewing thread, white
* 12½in (32 cm) wooden embroidery hoop
* 13 x 13in (33 x 33cm) piece of cardboard
* 10in (25cm) of ½in (1cm) wide ribbon

Finished size approx: 12½in (32 cm) diameter

1 Transfer the design on pages 52–53 (see Transferring a Design) on to the centre of the linen fabric.

2 Stitch the design using a back stitch and red cotton à broder with the chenille needle. Work the eyes of all the characters and animals with French knots, make cross stitches for the gingerbread man's buttons, and star stitch where shown on the design (see Essential Stitches).

3 Cut the square of embroidered fabric into a rough circle and, with double thread, use a knot and three stitches on top of each other to fasten on.

You can paint your wooden embroidery hoop any colour, but I chose red to match the redwork stitchery.

Mandy's Top Tips

4 Sew a row of gathering (running) stitches all around the outside edge with white sewing thread.

5 Trace the outside of the embroidery hoop with the screw on it onto cardboard, cut this circle out.

6 Place the work onto the embroidery hoop without the screw, making sure the design is central within the hoop. Place the hoop with the screw on over the slightly smaller hoop with the work attached, and tighten up the screw. You may need to tweak the work evenly around

the hoop at this point until it is smooth, making sure as you do so that you do not distort the design. Tighten up the screw again, making sure the fabric in the hoop is taut.

7 Pull your gathering stitches up tight and fasten off. Tie your ribbon to the top of the hoop and it's ready to hang. Glue the edge of the cardboard circle to the back of the wooden hoop to cover the reverse of the work.

Techniques
and Stitches

Fabric, Thread + Essentials

A good quality natural fabric is a pleasure to work with, and my ever-growing collection contains a wide variety of linens, cottons, calicos and felts that I've chosen because they feel lovely in the hand and are a joy to stitch. If you can comfortably slide a needle through it, I'll stitch it! I feel the same way about threads, and for all the projects in this book I've used a gorgeous coton à broder for the embroidery and good quality cotton thread for machine stitching. Build your own stash by keeping an eye out wherever you go, and never try to resist the urge to pick up quality fabric, thread, buttons, ribbons and other embellishments. You might miss something special!

Cottons and linens

I don't just rely on brand new fabrics for my collection, but relish trawling through second-hand shops with an eye to recycling vintage clothes, tray cloths and linens whenever I find something irresistible. I've even been known to 're-purpose' things from my own wardrobe. When I do visit quilt shops (and it's really important to support your local one), I like to buy bolt ends and off-cuts to boost my stash.

Before you begin

Give your fabrics a wash, and press them before you start stitching. You'll find out if there's any danger of the colour running or major shrinkage before any of your work is ruined. It's a good idea to give the fabrics a light spray of starch when pressing them, as this will make them easier to sew.

Coton à broder

I've used coton à broder throughout this book, and it's a real a favourite of mine for redwork. It is a single strand thread with a matt finish. Use it straight off the skein, without attempting to divide it into strands – it isn't the same as embroidery floss. I use no.16 width, which is quite thick and perfect for redwork and hand quilting. You should be able to find a good red coton à broder in quilting a craft shops, or we always have lots online at dandeliondesigns.co.uk.

I also love to use Aurifil 12 for work with finer details or for those who are more experienced and sew with a finer stitch. My favourite colours are 321 for coton à broder and 2250 for Aurifil.

Needles

Choose good-quality needles – you'll be glad you did! I've used chenille no.24 needles for the embroidery in this book as they work well with coton à broder. They are sharp, which allows them to glide through the fabric, and have a large eye, which will help to prevent frustration when you thread them. If you struggle with threading needles, try using a needle threader, or go up a size. My rule of thumb is that if a needle won't thread after three attempts, pick a larger one.

Spray adhesive

I always use spray adhesive (the kind that is especially designed for quilting) on small projects, it saves so much time compared with tacking or pinning. You just spray your wadding lightly with the adhesive, then smooth your work on top. Always spray the wadding or backing but never the embroidery! Because the adhesive is tacky you can peel off and reposition it. Please read the instructions on the can for health and safety advice.

Transferring a Design

Pencil

For fabrics you can see through, this is my preferred method for transferring a design. Just place your fabric over the template and use either a well-sharpened pencil or a good quality propelling pencil to mark the design onto the fabric. The pencil lines will be so fine that they will not require erasing. It is possible to find a propelling pencil with different coloured leads, which will be visible on darker fabrics. Alternatively try a water colour pencil for different coloured fabrics – you can choose any colour of pencil, light or dark, that contrasts well with your fabric, and the marks can be washed out by rubbing with a damp cotton bud.

Dressmaker's pencil

Specially designed for marking fabric, these pencils are readily available in quilting and craft shops. They come in various colours, making them suitable for light or dark fabrics. You won't be able to sharpen a dressmaker's pencil so easily, but the marks are simple to brush or wash off.

Iron-on transfer pencil

This specialist pencil's marks are permanent, so you'll need to cover them up with your stitching. It's therefore essential to keep your marks fine by regularly sharpening the pencil. This method is useful for fabrics that you cannot see through such as felt. To avoid a mirror image of the motif, make your first tracing with an ordinary pencil, then re-trace the design onto another sheet of tracing paper using the iron-on transfer pencil. Next, place the tracing paper onto your fabric, right sides together and press (without steam). The pencil marks will transfer onto your fabric.

Pens

Choose between fade-away, washable or permanent pens – each one has its pros and cons. The marks of a fade-away pen work well on light fabrics and don't need to be washed off, but may fade before you have finished stitching. Also, never iron fade-away pen marks or expose them to heat as they may become permanent or leave a stain. Washable pens can be erased by washing (as the name suggests) or by dabbing with a damp cotton bud, but test on your fabric first as these too can stain. Use permanent pens for the accurate stitching of very detailed embroidery. It is, however, very permanent so your stitching will need to cover it up.

Dressmaker's carbon paper

This stuff works just like regular carbon paper: place the paper on the fabric, right sides together, put the tracing or template on top and draw around the design to transfer it. Work on a hard flat surface, tape the fabric down so that it doesn't move and press very firmly with a ball point pen. The transferred line can be quite thick and might not come out successfully. On the plus side, the paper is available in white, blue, pink and yellow, so should mark all fabric colours.

Light box

A light box is great for tracing designs onto pale fabrics. The light will shine through the fabric and the template, so you can clearly see where to trace. Light boxes are not very expensive, although you can make your own with a strong box, with a light fitting inside and a piece of clear perspex on top. Alternatively, just tape the template to a window, hold or tape your fabric on top, and trace it off.

Essential Stitches

BACK STITCH

This is the stitch to use for creating the clear lines of all of the stitched designs in this book.

Start

Work from right to left, and make your stitches small and of an equal length. Bring the needle up a little ahead of where you want the line of stitching to start. Take the needle to the right, to the start position (shown on the diagram), back through the fabric to make a stitch, and then bring it out to the left of the first stitch. Each time a stitch is made, the thread passes back to fill the gap.

   If you are left-handed, make the stitch in the same way, but work from left to right. Practice will make your stitches neat and even, but a slightly uneven stitch can look appealing too.

FRENCH KNOT

A perfect stitch for dots and spots and for Reindeer eyes!

Bring the needle through from the back of the fabric, and wrap the thread around the needle two or three times. Push the needle back into the fabric very close to where it originally came out, but not through exactly the same hole or your knot will not happen!

   Gently pull up the thread that is twisted around the needle before pushing the needle back through the fabric. Place your fingernail over the twist of thread as you pull the needle through. You can make the French knot larger or smaller by wrapping the thread around the needle more or fewer times.

CROSS STITCH

Whole designs are often stitched in cross stitch, but in this book we're using it scattered about for a little decoration.

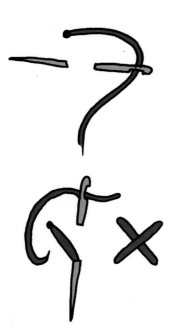

Work from left to right, creating a little cross in an imaginary square. Bring the needle up through the fabric at your start point. Make a stitch diagonally from the top left to the bottom right, then bring the needle back out at the lower left corner. Next make a stitch to the top right corner and bring the needle back where the next cross stitch is required. Pull the needle through to complete the cross stitch.

   If you are left-handed, work from right to left, making your first diagonal stitch from top right to bottom left, and the second one from bottom right to top left.

Star stitch

A star stitch is worked just like a cross stitch, but with two more stitches to make a star rather than a simple cross. It's basically a cross stitch on top of a cross stitch. Follow the instructions for cross stitch to make the two crossing diagonal stitches, then add a vertical one and a horizontal one. You might to make each stitch a little longer than you would when making a cross stitch, to allow room for those extra stitches.

CHAIN STITCH

A lovely stitch, and very versatile as it's easy to adapt for a variety of effects. It's ideal for surface decoration and even quilting as it leaves a straight stitch on the back.

To start, bring the needle and thread right up from the back of your work, through to the front. Put the needle back in from the front of the fabric, by the side of the first stitch, placing it a short distance away. Place the thread under your needle and pull the needle and thread through the first stitch. Repeat, making sure you always start each new stitch within the loop of the last one.

LADDER STITCH

For closing a slit, or the gap in a seam used for stuffing, ladder stitch is ideal. It's name comes from the way the stitches look like a ladder until you pull them tight to close the seam.

Knot the end of the thread and start from inside the opening to hide the knot. Make straight stitches into the folded fabric, stitching into each edge in turn. After a few stitches pull the thread taut to draw up the stitches and close the gap.

SINGLE CHAIN STITCH AND LAZY DAISY STITCH
Make a single chain stitch, as described above, or complete a circle of lazy daisy stitches to make little flowers.

Bring your needle up from the back of the fabric at your start point. Leaving a little loop of thread insert the needle back into the fabric very close to your start point. Bring the needle up through the fabric again at the opposite end of your loop, making sure the looped thread stays under the needle. Finish by making a little stitch over the loop to hold it in place, and then bring your needle up from the back of the fabric where you want to start the next lazy daisy stitch.

SLIP STITCH
Slip stitch is used to sew binding (or the borders of the placemats) to the wrong side of the work.

You will need to use ordinary sewing thread that matches your fabric and a household sewing needle – this is not a decorative stitch so you don't want it to show. Take a small pinch of the fabric and slip the needle into the binding, pull the needle through and repeat.

BLANKET STITCH
I love this stitch for edging and borders, and I use it a lot for appliqué.

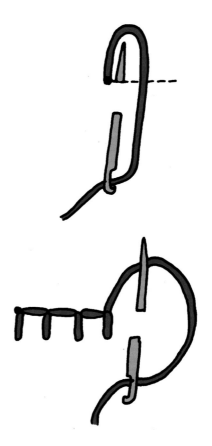

Working from left to right, start by bringing the needle up on the line of the template you are following, or the edge of the appliqué, or very close to the raw edge of the fabric you are covering. Take a stitch down from this point and bring the needle back where you started, keeping your thread to the left. Then insert the needle to the right of the first stitch, down a little from the line or edge, and bring it back out on the line or edge, making sure the thread is behind the needle. Pull through. Repeat to make a line of stitches, always aiming to keep the tops of the stitches level. If you are left-handed work this stitch in the opposite direction, from right to left.

RUNNING STITCH

Like the name suggests, you just run the needle in and out of the fabric to make a simple line of stitches. You can use a running stitch for gathering fabric, as you will need to do when assembling the hoopies.

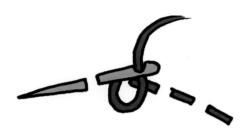

You can make your line of stitches straight or curved, or even a circle if needed. Work from right to left, bringing your needle up through the fabric to make a stitch, and then bringing the needle down through the fabric again. Repeat, making sure the stitches and the spaces between them are the same size. If you are left-handed follow these instructions but just work from left to right. If you are working this as a gathering stitch, make your stitches and the gaps between them a little longer.

STEM STITCH

This is just perfect for outlining, although you might find it's not plain sailing for going around sharp corners.

FEATHER STITCH

I find it really useful when stitching feather stitch to have an imaginary line running through the middle of it to keep it straight.

Start at the end of your imaginary line and put the needle in 1/8in (3mm) to the right and up from the start position. Pop the needle out on the imaginary line 1/8in (3mm) straight up from the start, the thread will be under the needle. Now make a stitch from the left side in the same way.

TOP STITCHING

This is a machine sewing technique to decorate or emphasize a seam or edge.
Set your machine to a straight stitch. Work from the right side. Use the edge of your machine foot as a guide and stitch close to the seam. You can use the width of the foot to sew a parallel seam close to the first, much like the seam on a pair of jeans.

Acknowledgements

Over the years I have met a wonderful team of people who help me put these amazing books together, without them it would not be possible to create such lovely work, I do so love what I make, and without them I cannot share with you my designs.

So huge thanks and hugs go to Ali Myer and her book designing skills and her very lovely side kick Jane Trollope, who actually launched my writing career, way back in the day. A huge thank you to Sian who continues to take the most beautiful photos of my home and samples for this book.

My back bones, Andee, Mel and Vicki, who are solely responsible for the smooth running of Dandelion Designs. Andee is efficient and organised and keeps our office running smoothly, Mel deals with all the orders and puts together the kits and answers all your questions and queries, Vicki fills in all the gaps but excels at computer skills and never raises her eye brows when I ask her the most basic of questions. Jenny takes away car boots full of fabric and brings back gorgeous packaged kits, while lovely Iris helps me out with the Redwork when my hands give up. You girls are invaluable to me and I send to you a huge thank you.

But most importantly, my drive and inspiration comes from my most beautiful family that is growing larger by the year and at the head of this lovely bunch is Mr Shaw. He supports me in everything I do, at a push he is even known to cut up yards and yards of fabric for kits, this is a big ask as he is a woodsman, what a dream!

A Dandelion Design Publications Book
© Mandy Shaw 2019
www.dandeliondesigns.co.uk

978-0-9957509-3-7

Text, Photography and Design © Mandy Shaw 2019

First published in 2019

Mandy Shaw has asserted the right to be identified as author of this work in accordance with the Copyright, Designs and Patents Act, 1988

Printed in the UK by Brightsea Print Group
for Dandelion Designs Ltd
37 Summerheath Road, Hailsham, BN27 3DS

Index

Dandeliondesigns.co.uk

You can buy all the fabric, Mandy's favourite Coton à Broder, threads, ribbons and buttons you need to make the projects in this book and much, much more at Mandy Shaw's very own online store

Dandeliondesigns.co.uk

Celebrate your love of Redwork and Christmas with this wonderful collection of Festive Redwork Projects from award winning designer Mandy Shaw.

Illustrated throughout with stunning photography, shot in Mandy's own home, all projects have step-by-step instructions and full size templates.

Dandelion Designs Publications

ISBN 978-0-9957509-3-7

£12.99

9 780995 750937